Dress Up Zendaya

ILLUSTRATED BY
JULIA MURRAY

Dress Up Zendaya

A ZENDAYA
PAPER DOLL BOOK
FEATURING HER
MOST ICONIC
LOOKS

Smith
Street
Books

Instructions

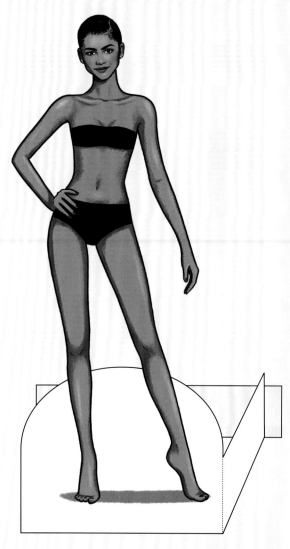

TO USE, CAREFULLY PRESS OUT THE DOLL
AND CROSS-PIECE AND ASSEMBLE THE
STAND AS SHOWN BELOW.

PRESS OUT THE OUTFITS AND GET DRESSING.
DRESS ZENDAYA IN HER ICONIC LOOKS
OR TRY MIXING AND MATCHING.

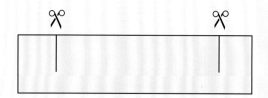

USE SCISSORS TO SNIP THE
CROSS-PIECE AND STAND

SLOT CROSS-PIECE INTO THE FLAPS

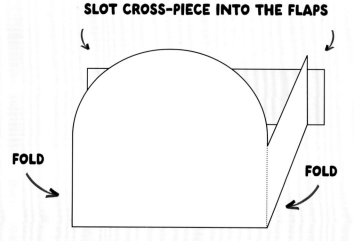

FOLD

FOLD

FOLD TABS
TO SECURE

Met Gala: "Heavenly Bodies"

2018

CUSTOM ATELIER VERSACE
"JEANNE D'ARC" CHAINMAIL,
ARMOR, AND SEQUINED GOWN,
PAIRED WITH JIMMY CHOO
"MAX" PLATFORM HEELS AND
TIFFANY & CO. JEWELRY.

STYLED BY LAW ROACH.

Vanity Fair & Lancôme Toast Women in Hollywood

2018

MARC JACOBS FALL 2018 COLOR-BLOCK ZOOT SUIT WITH A WIDE-BRIM BOATER AND ORANGE POINTED-TOE HEELS.

STYLED BY LAW ROACH.

Emmy Awards

2020

CUSTOM GIORGIO ARMANI PRIVE GOWN WITH A BEJEWELED BUSTIER AND POLKA-DOT SKIRT, PAIRED WITH BULGARI JEWELRY.

STYLED BY LAW ROACH.

Critics' Choice Awards

2020

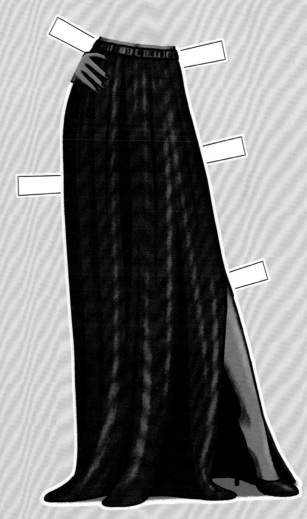

CUSTOM VERSION OF TOM FORD SPRING 2020 LACQUERED FUCHSIA BREAST PLATE AND MAXI SKIRT WITH CHRISTIAN LOUBOUTIN "IRIZA" PUMPS.

STYLED BY LAW ROACH.

Venice Film Festival

2021

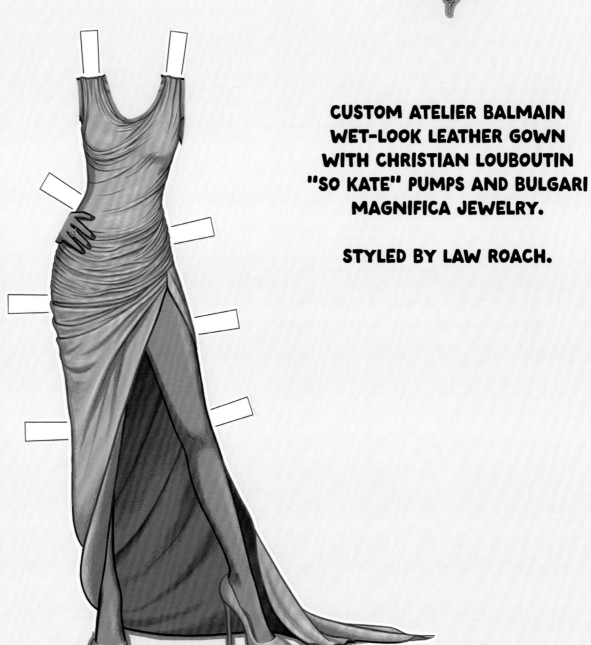

CUSTOM ATELIER BALMAIN WET-LOOK LEATHER GOWN WITH CHRISTIAN LOUBOUTIN "SO KATE" PUMPS AND BULGARI MAGNIFICA JEWELRY.

STYLED BY LAW ROACH.

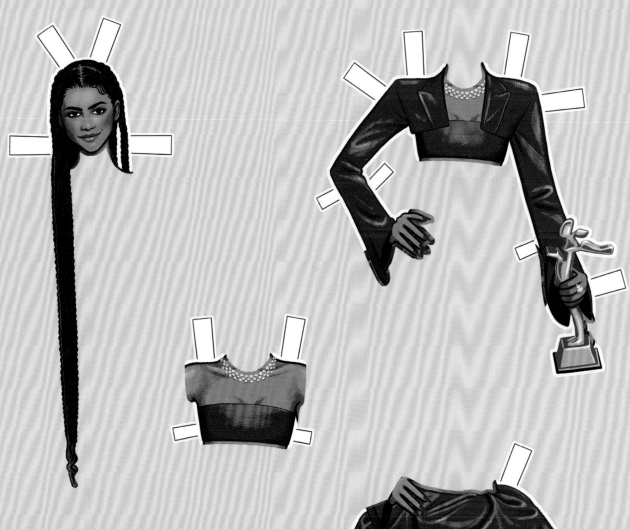

CFDA
Awards

2021

CUSTOM VERA WANG HAUTE COUTURE CRIMSON SILK FAILLE COLUMN SKIRT WITH BUBBLE DETAIL, BANDEAU, AND CROPPED JACKET WITH JIMMY CHOO HEELS, AND BULGARI JEWELRY.

STYLED BY LAW ROACH.

Spider-Man: No Way Home LA Premiere

2021

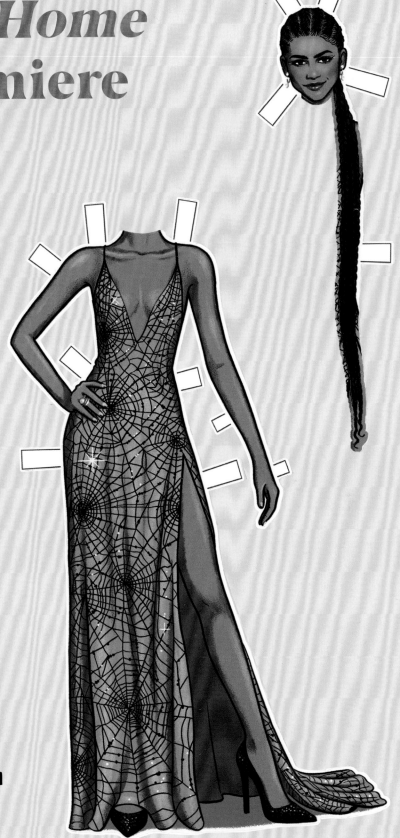

CUSTOM ATELIER VALENTINO SPIDERWEB DRESS, PIERPAOLO PICCIOLI BLACK FEATHERED MASK, CHRISTIAN LOUBOUTIN BLACK CRYSTAL PUMPS, AND BULGARI JEWELRY.

STYLED BY LAW ROACH.

Vanity Fair
Oscars
Afterparty
2022

SPORTMAX FALL 2022
DOUBLE-BREASTED
HOURGLASS SUIT, PLUM
SHIRT, AND LEATHER TIE,
PAIRED WITH JIMMY CHOO
"MAX" PLATFORMS AND
BULGARI JEWELRY.

STYLED BY LAW ROACH.

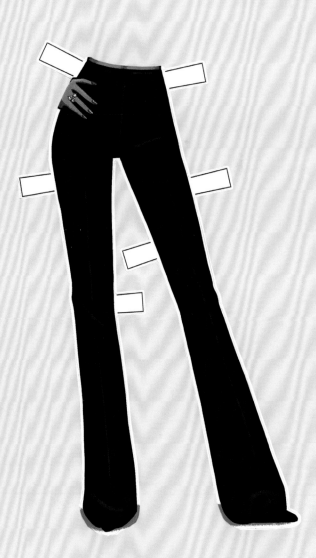

Valentino Show

2022

VALENTINO FALL 2022
FUCHSIA BLOUSE,
TWO-PIECE SUIT WITH
FLORAL APPLIQUES,
AND OVERCOAT WITH
VALENTINO GARAVANI
PLATFORM HEELS.

STYLED BY
LAW ROACH.

Dune: Part Two London Premiere

2024

THIERRY MUGLER FALL 1995
CHROME AND PLEXIGLASS
GYNOID BODYSUIT, CO-DESIGNED
BY JEAN-JACQUES URCUN.

STYLED BY LAW ROACH.

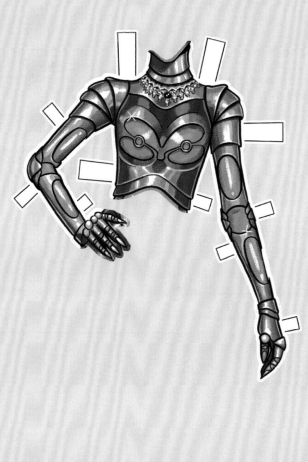

Challengers Rome Photocall

2024

CUSTOM LOEWE SILVER
DROP-WAIST DRESS AND
TENNIS BALL HEELS, PAIRED
WITH BULGARI JEWELRY.

STYLED BY LAW ROACH.

Met Gala: "The Garden of Time"

2024

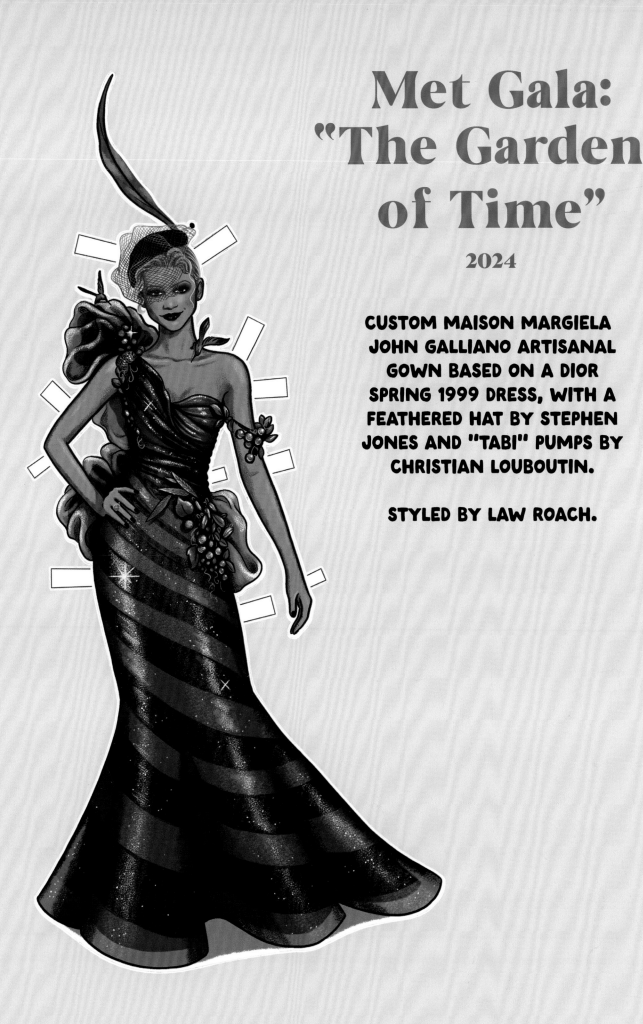

CUSTOM MAISON MARGIELA JOHN GALLIANO ARTISANAL GOWN BASED ON A DIOR SPRING 1999 DRESS, WITH A FEATHERED HAT BY STEPHEN JONES AND "TABI" PUMPS BY CHRISTIAN LOUBOUTIN.

STYLED BY LAW ROACH.

Published in 2025 by Smith Street Books
Naarm (Melbourne) | Australia
smithstreetbooks.com

ISBN: 978-1-9232-3906-7

Smith Street Books respectfully acknowledges the Wurundjeri People of the
Kulin Nation, who are the Traditional Owners of the land on which we work,
and we pay our respects to their Elders past and present.

Publisher: Hannah Koelmeyer
Editor: Lucy Grant
Illustrator: Julia Murray
Design and layout: Alissa Dinallo
Production manager: Aisling Coughlan
Proofreader: Ariana Klepac
Prepress: Megan Ellis

Printed & bound in China by C&C Offset Printing Co., Ltd.

Book 380
10 9 8 7 6 5 4 3 2 1

Please note: This title is not affiliated with or endorsed in any way
by Zendaya. We are just big fans.